Big Truck, Big Trouble

By
Stan Surbrook

PUBLISHED by PARABLES
Earthly Stories with a Heavenly Meaning

Big Truck, Big Trouble
By Stan Surbrook

Published By Parables
July 2021

All Rights Reserved. No part of this book may be reproduced or utilized in any form or by any means, electronic or mechanical, including photocopying, **recording, or by any information storage and retrieval system, without permission in writing from the author.**

Printed in the United States of America

Readers should be aware that Internet Web sites offered as citations and/or sources for further information may have been changed or disappeared between the time this was written and the time it is read.

Big Truck, Big Trouble

By
Stan Surbrook

Dedication

I dedicate this book to my precious wife, Ronda:

I could never have done half the things "right" in my life if it had not been for the love of my wife. It is not an easy thing to be married to a cop, fireman, or UPS man like me who is gone all night long. I worked 60 hours every week. It takes a very special wife to deal with that! To God be the glory, Amen.

And to my loving daughter, Lisa:

During the early years of this book, Lisa gave me countless ideas and encouraged me when I got burned out. She is a wonderful Daughter and mother to my grandkids; truly a "father's daughter."

Stan Surbrook

As he rounded the last corner on Turner's grade, Hal slid the heaters' control knob a couple of clicks to the right for just a little more heat. From up here, he could look down on the lights of the city below. The early morning air was cool and moist. This was the spot he waited for every night, because he knew in an hour or so he would pull the big rig into the terminal's entrance, and his next stop would be home.

For over twenty-five years this is how Hal Dalstrom had made his living. He would drive all night across the state, through the plains, and over the mountains. Then, he would exchange trailers at an exchange point and head back east over the mountains and be back again to greet the early dawn light and the place he called home.

It was the last major city that rested on the Washington Idaho state line. Of course, from here, Canada is only about 100 miles to

Big Truck, Big Trouble

the North, and the great state of Montana is a mere 75 miles further east. It was the perfect place to have a "line-haul" trucking business, and Hal started working for the company as soon as he got out of the service. Which is where he spent 2 years in the Marines and did his time in Vietnam.

He had tried a few different jobs when he got out of the Marine Corps, but the 'road' was his heart's choice. However on this morning, he was more than just tired. His heart felt heavy. It was like he wanted to say something but had no words to form his thoughts.

What a strange feeling he had inside. Who would have guessed that a simple cup of coffee at the all-night café would have sparked such feelings? What he really wished he could do was to forget the whole thing, but it kept playing over and over in his head like re-runs from an old TV series. Anyway, where did that guy get off sticking his nose in my business and asking me such a question. It's not that Hal did not believe in God, it's just that there are some things a person does not talk about, let alone in public. And what did he mean, "someday all the earth will stand in the presence of God publicly, and God will read of their life's work and judge accordingly?"

Still, he could not help feeling there was something to all this stuff. Oh sure, he had run across those 'religious kooks' before and some very strange things had happened over the years. Like that one night, Hal recalled, back in the winter of '73; during one of those nights that you try to forget, snowin' like there's no tomorrow. It seemed like that guy came out of nowhere, he remembered. Hal had pulled off the highway and was installing tire chains when the big rig slid backwards about an inch on the ice. That was

Big Truck, Big Trouble

just enough to pin Hal's jacket sleeve under the drive tires. That guy helped him get out of that 'little mess' Just in the right time. "Yeah, that sure was some good luck," Hal thought. But when he turned to thank him, the guy said, "your Heavenly Father loves you very much." Hal did not know what to say except to offer to buy him a cup of coffee, but when he turned back at him, the guy was gone. Just as quickly as he appeared, he was gone. "He must have stopped to chain-up his own rig; just happened by," Hal thought.

Then there was the time he came across that van load of church kids that slid off the road and hit a tree. "Man, did that thing burst into flames," Hal remembered. He usually stopped at the diner for a coffee about eight o'clock, before heading up the pass, but that night he missed the exit. His mind was drifting as he remembered the way he had spoken to his sweet, little wife, Annie. They had been married for twenty-six years, and she had been the best thing that ever happened to him. He never meant to hurt her, and he was ashamed for what he had said.

His mind became focused again as he realized what appeared in the windshield was an accident. He yanked his cell phone off the dash and quickly dialed 911 and called for help. Then, he grabbed his gloves and flashlight and ran across the freeway and down the steep embankment. As he got closer, he could see flames near the front of the van and realized it was only a matter of minutes before it would explode. Hal emptied the contents of his fire extinguisher, but it barely made a dent in the fire. Another rig pulled up, and Hal yelled, "grab your fire extinguisher," but Hal knew he had to get those kids out fast. When he turned back toward the rear of the van, he noticed there was one very tall and stout man that apparently had gotten out of the

Big Truck, Big Trouble

crash unscathed. He and Hal wrestled with the back door of the van finally popping it open, then frantically pulling the kids to safety. There were eight kids altogether, plus the driver, and Hal shuttered to think what he would have come across, had he been just a few minutes later.

"Are you alright?" Hal asked the driver, exhausted.

"Yes, we're fine, but if you had not helped us get that door open, we would have been toast," the driver said.

But Hal quickly added, "Yeah, but without the help of your friend here, I could never have got that door open by myself."

The driver answered, "There were just the kids and me, sir."

Hal looked around and noticed the guy with the fire extinguisher had just arrived and the other onlookers were still up on the roadway. "Well, somebody was here," Hal said defensively, "and you sure were lucky."

"It's not luck, friend," the man said, "I'm a pastor, and I know the hand of the Lord was upon us."

Hal finished the paperwork with the state patrol and hurried on his way. "Sure is a funny thing," he thought. "Wait 'til Annie hears about this," he said to himself as he brought the big rig back up to speed. Hal searched his mind for other incidents that had happened like that over the many years and countless miles, the ones with strange circumstances, as he drove along that night.

But he quickly forgot about the whole thing as he approached the front gate and guard shack at the terminal's entrance. Hal rolled down the window and barked, "Morning, Bill," in his usual raspy voice.

Big Truck, Big Trouble

"Morning, Hal," the guard said. "The dispatcher wants you to put your trailers on door five and door six."

"You got it," Hal replied.

The afternoon sun was peeking through the cracks around the window shades and blinds that Hal had installed in the bedroom window. Annie was a great homemaker, and she had fixed up their little cottage so nice. She really did not like the way Hal had made their bedroom "into a dungeon," but knew how hard it was to sleep in the daytime. Annie had worked plenty of nights herself in her volunteer work at the hospital. She and Hal had first met there one night when Hal had rushed a man to the emergency room after being hurt in the terminal's massive loading docks.

Hal was a sound sleeper, but the smell of Annie's homemade biscuits would wake him every time. "Man, I love that woman,"

Hal thought as he forced his eyelids open. The light from the kitchen made it hard to see, but he quickly found Annie's smiling face and gave her a respectable peck on the cheek. "What's a guy gotta do around here to get a little grub?" Hal asked jokingly.

"Flirt with the cook," Annie fired back at him.

"Well, I'm afraid my wife wouldn't like that very much." They both smiled and seemed to enjoy the simple humor.

"I'll have your breakfast ready in a little bit," she said, "but in the meantime, would you fix the faucet in the bathroom?"

Hal had his whole body in the bathroom cabinet and wished he were still sleeping. Plumbing had never really made it to the top of his "ten favorite things to do" list. It's just that a good plumber needs to be limber, small framed, and good with his hands. All qualities that had eluted Hal. He

Big Truck, Big Trouble

was overweight, clumsy, and slightly short of patience, or so he had been told.

Hal had his right hand crammed behind the pipes that lead to the faucet and was about to conquer the beast, when he heard, "Hal, your breakfast is ready, and the phone is for you." He raised up and smacked his head on the bottom of the sink and let out a yelp, followed by a few "not so choice" words.

"Hal Dalstrom," Annie barked, "you know I don't want to hear that kind of talk in this home." Annie was a Christian woman and very active in her church. Hal decided the plumbing job would have to wait until the weekend, when he might have a few less interruptions and a little more patience. Annie did not argue the point with him either.

"Who is it, and what do they want?" Hal snorted as he walked past Annie to pick up the phone. "Hello, this is Hal, what can I do for 'ya?" he said into the mouthpiece.

"Hal," the voice on the line said, "this is Raymond down at the terminal. I'm sorry to bother you at home," he apologized, "but something's come up, and I wanted to talk to you about it." Hal stood up straight and with a deep voice said, "yeah, go ahead." Hal was not a proud man, but he was no one's fool either. Twice he had been awarded Road Driver of the Year and once the National Safety Council's award for heroism. Hal had pulled a trucker from his overturned, burning rig. Hal was senior driver at Cascade Transport and had worked there nearly thirty years.

"We got a special load here, Hal," the dispatcher continued, "and we were wondering if you could help us out."

"Well, what's up?" Hal responded.

Big Truck, Big Trouble

"This is a load to be delivered way back in the sticks," Raymond said. "It's not a good road, Hal. The agent said there's still a lot of snow up there."

"Story of my life," Hal said jokingly. "So when's this supposed to go?"

"We'll talk about it when you get here," the dispatcher said, and then, hung up.

"What was that all about?" Annie asked.

"Oh, just Raymond wantin' to send me off a cliff," Hal said sarcastically. Raymond and Hal didn't exactly have a 'cozy' relationship. Actually, they had been at odds for years. Raymond was another one of those 'fanatical Christians' that seemed to plague Hal everywhere he went. Besides that, he was a dispatcher, and that meant he was management, and that meant he was "out to get" the hourly employees, or at least in Hal's eyes it did.

Stan Surbrook

It was a quarter past four when Hal wheeled his four-wheel drive pickup into the employee' parking area. He turned right to the front of the lot and found his usual space. One of the younger drivers had affectionately hung a sign on the fence that read "the Old Goat's Spot". He walked past the gate guard and forced out the words to say, "How 'ya doin', John?"

He climbed the long, steel staircase and gave a twist to the knob on the door of the dispatch office, and immediately made eye contact with Raymond. "Oh, there you are," Raymond said with a smile.

"Yeah, here I are," Hal said sarcastically.

Raymond just gave a little shake to his head and said, "It looks like that load I told you about needs to go on Saturday."

"Saturday, why Saturday?" Hal asked.

Big Truck, Big Trouble

"The guys will be hooking it up Monday morning, and because it's so expensive, they didn't want it there until they're ready to start. I told them there was no way we could deliver it on Sunday, so they agreed to have it delivered on Saturday. A technician will meet you there and get it mounted and ready to go for the crew on Monday morning," Raymond said. Hal knew he'd have to get started early Saturday morning in order to be up there by seven.

As dispatchers do, he didn't tell Hal all the details concerning this 'very special' cargo. "Are my trailers ready to go?" Hal interrupted, as he turned to look out of the glass enclosed dispatch office.

"Almost, Hal, but let's go over the plan for Saturday," Raymond said.

But Hal cut him off short and said, "we'll worry about Saturday when Saturday gets here. Right now, I just want to get out of here, and get on the road man."

Raymond sensed something was bothering him and said, "Hal, you know me and you have never been real close, but if you ever need someone to listen, or maybe pray with you, I'd consider it an honor."

"Spare me," Hal snapped back. But as he grabbed the door handle, he looked back at Raymond and said "uh, thanks anyway, Ray."

That was the first time in the fifteen years he had worked with Hal, that he acted like he cared what Raymond thought. Raymond wondered what was going through the mind of this gray-haired warrior of the road, but he knew when to back off.

As usual, the phone in the dispatch office was ringing off the hook as it did that time of the day. But when Raymond answered the next call, he realized it was Annie on the

Big Truck, Big Trouble

line, and she said, "Hi, Raymond. Has Hal left yet?"

"He just pulled out, Annie," Raymond said.

"Oh boy…he forgot his medicine, and I know he'll need it later," she said.

"What, for his arthritis?" Raymond asked. "No the other stuff he takes, for the nausea, Ray," Annie said.

"What's this? The 'ol guy gets carsick now?" Raymond asked.

"The chemo makes him sick to his stomach, Ray," Annie said.

Suddenly, Raymond realized that Hal had been hiding this from him.

"Annie, I'm afraid I don't know what you're talking about," Raymond said.

"Hal has a spot on his lung that showed up last spring when he had such a bad cold, Ray," Annie said. "But the doctors said that it would be okay after a few rounds of chemo."

Now Raymond understood why Hal had been so grumpy lately. "Poor, 'ol guy," Raymond thought. "He's trying to carry this thing himself."

Saturday morning, well before dawn, Hal wheeled into the drivers parking lot after picking up some donuts. Even though the only car in the lot was Raymond's blazer, he pulled into the spot where the little sign the drivers had hung on the fence was. That stupid little sign always got a grin out of him. Raymond had the coffee on, and Hal could smell it clear out on the dock as he made his way up the long staircase to the dispatch office. "Morning, Ray," Hal said with a smile.

Raymond spun around with such a jolt that he nearly knocked the dozen donuts that Hal was carrying out of his hands. "Whoa,

Big Truck, Big Trouble

you're in a good mood this morning," Raymond said with surprise.

"Well, I feel good, and I'm still breathin', 'ya know?" Hal said with a ring in his voice. Raymond knew Hal was speaking literally because he understood what Hal meant. But he wouldn't let on that he really knew.

"You know, Hal, if you know where you're goin' after this life, you can have that peaceful feeling all the time. But I know you don't want to hear about that stuff," Raymond said gracefully.

"Yeah, I know Ray. That's what my Annie is always telling me." Hal said that with a kinder tone than Ray had noticed in the past.

"My offer's always there, if you ever want to talk about it Hal," Raymon said.

"Let's get down to business here. Are they done loading my trailer? I want to get on the road, man," Hal said impatiently.

"Yeah, they're done and gone home, and I was just finishing the bill of lading and the hazardous papers."

"Hazardous…I thought this was a transmitter for some Christian radio station?" Hal asked.

"It is" Hal, but this is no ordinary transmitter. They have been building it for six months. That baby's got enough power to beam signals through solid rock. It's nuclear powered and can run for weeks on the solar back-up power supply." Ray sounded like he was part owner in the thing, and actually, he was.

"So, that's the one all that fund-raising stuff was goin' on about this summer, huh?" Hal asked.

"Yes, Hal, it's completely paid for, and the land it will sit on is leased from the forest service for ninety-nine years."

Big Truck, Big Trouble

"Well, what are you gonna do after the lease is up, bring it back down?" Hal retorted.

"That's why the spot where it will sit is so remote and hard to get into, Hal. "It'll set on one of the highest peaks around, beaming out the 'good news' for hundreds of miles." Raymond's voice was singing now.

"Oh, brother," Hal said, shaking his head.

"It won't be an easy delivery, Hal. Bonnie and I took a drive up there last Sunday after church and had to lock-in the hubs on the blazer just to get in there. What's not covered with snow is deep in mud. That's why we wanted you to deliver it, Hal."

After a couple cups of coffee and two jelly-filled doughnuts, Hal tipped his baseball cap to Raymond and pulled his rig out of the terminal heading towards the freeway on-ramp. There was little traffic for a Saturday morning, but Hal drove the same way he always did, safely and courteously, but determined. He took great pride in always being on schedule. He would stop about thirty miles out, near the old copper mine to check the load and the tires before the long trip across the prairie to the cascades.

Along the way he knew he would be meeting his other truckers buddies that made the trip from East to West and back again Monday through Friday. Hal worked Sunday night through Thursday night, so he would really surprise those guys when he came within 'two-way radio range' of them. It had been years since Hal had worked a Saturday. That's the day he usually did his yard work, and spent Sunday working on his old car in the shop he had built out back. Hal never was much of a drinker, but he did keep some beer in the little refrigerator in his shop.

Big Truck, Big Trouble

He had smoked for years but quit last spring when they found the spot on his lung. The chemotherapy kept him from drinking any alcohol, so he just kept it around for his buddies.

Hal enjoyed talking on the C.B. radio because he never felt that far away from the ones he knew in the industry, and especially so, during the foul weather that many times he had to fight. Just then he heard the radio crack, "Hey, how 'bout that Cascade transport truck over there going West. You got a copy?"

Hal recognized his old friend, Birk Adams, and was smiling as he grabbed the microphone and answered, "Just who wants to know?" Hal fired back.

"Well, I'll be dipped," Birk said. "It's Papa Dalstrom."

"Hey, Birk. Who 'ya got runnin' with you over there this morning?" Hal asked.

"Oh, Sparky and Richard, and the Fedex boys are back there bringing up the rear."

Then Hal answered back, "those guys are always bringing up the rear."

"Only because we got these stupid speed-limiters," came the reply from "Mule," one of the Fedex driver's.

"Well, Hal, I didn't think I'd ever see you working on a Saturday," Birk said with amazement.

"Oh, that simple dispatcher of mine is always making promises to somebody, and this one is gonna cost him time and a half," Hal said with authority.

"Well, what the heck are you hauling on that flatbed trailer, Hal?" Birk asked.

"It's a high powered satellite-transmitter for some Christian radio station," Hal said.

Big Truck, Big Trouble

"Well, praise the Lord," Birk said sarcastically.

"Yeah, well as long as they're signing my paycheck, I don't care what I'm hauling," Hal said. "I just want to get up there, get this thing off, and get back home."

Hal said good-bye to his friends who were going East, and wished he was going that way, too. But he knew he had a job to do first, so he mashed down on the throttle and chased the early morning dawning as he headed across the brush covered flatlands to the beautiful Cascade Mountain range. Hal loved this wide-open country and enjoyed the early morning air as he rolled down the window just a little.

It was almost six in the morning by the time he got to the little café at the foot of the pass. Verna was surprised to see her old pal since she started working days at the restaurant. "Well, Hal Dalstrom. What brings you up here in the light of day?" she asked.

"Throw on a couple of eggs and some good 'ol biscuits, and I'll tell you all about it," Hal said.

"You got it, Hal. How about some sausage too?" Verna asked.

One of the things a trucker learns fast is who has the best chow and the best prices. Attitude is optional, but it's a rare thing to find all three in one place. The Gateway Café was just that. And Verna was icing for the cake. She had lost her husband of forty-one years to a mine cave-in and stayed working at the diner for the small income she needed. Hal often slipped her a twenty-dollar bill when she wasn't looking. "Annie says the 'Good Book' tells us to watch out for the widows and orphans of this world", he used to tell his buddies. "And God blesses those that bless others," that was Hal's favorite.

Big Truck, Big Trouble

Forty-five minutes later, Hal was back in the truck and heading for the pass. But when he came to the "Railroad Canyon Road" exit, he turned off the interstate and headed up the steep, narrow road. It was kinda weird turning off the freeway at that exit because Hal realized he'd never been up that stretch of highway before. "Railroad Canyon Road" had simply been another one of many, many exits off the interstate that he had roared by over the years. Now, he was actually going into new territory. Hal thought about his life as the big rig struggled to build speed up the long grade. Funny, he thought, after all these years of routine driving East to West, then West to East, he was taking a different path. It was sort of refreshing, he thought.

"Maybe that's what retirement will be like," Hal thought to himself. When a guy spends so much time alone, mile after mile, you learn to carry on quite a conversation with yourself. And the best thing about dialoguing with yourself is that you always get the last word.

He and Annie had been discussing plans to retire lately, but the thought of it worried Hal. He didn't know anything but truck driving, and to sit around and watch TV all day, didn't do a thing for him. But somehow his heart was "talking" to him as he climbed higher and higher. He felt free from the trappings of "the same old grind."

The sun had already made its appearance as the "Forest Service Road 163" sign came into view. One thing about Raymond's dispatching was that he always took great care in giving directions to these 'special' unload points. Most dispatchers cannot even get the exit number right, but not Raymond. That's one thing even Hal would admit; Raymond was one good dispatcher.

Big Truck, Big Trouble

Hal took the corner wide so his trailer would clear the gate, using all of the two-lane paved road. The gate was open, and a pickup truck was waiting for Hal there. Hal pulled the parking brake and stepped out into the cool morning air. "Good morning," the man in the pickup said.

"Well, good morning to you, sir," Hal said.

"The name's Bruce Cotter. I'm with Satellite Systems of America," he said. "And you must be Hal Dalstrom."

"Well, yes, sir. I am," Hal said with a smile.

"I go to the same church your wife, Annie, and Raymond attend," he said.

"Huh, isn't that something," Hal answered. "So how far is it up there anyway?" Hal asked.

"Well, this good road goes for about a mile or so…"

"Good road?" Hal interrupted, "if you call this a good road, I can't wait to see the 'bad part'."

"Yeah, I know, but the piece of ground we got…I mean, it's just perfect to set the transmitter on," Bruce said.

"So, you just follow me, and we'll take it real slow and easy. There's a road that branches off the main road about a mile or so down from the top; it used to lead to some old silver mine. The earthquake last year caused a huge slide, and the road drops off more than a hundred feet straight down. I'd hate to think what would happen if somebody was to drive off that cliff," said Bruce.

"Well, if it's all the same to you Bruce, I'd like to get this over with and get back to the house. This is Saturday, man, and I don't usually work on Saturdays," Hal said.

"Yep, I'm with you Hal, my wife Holly, is about to have our first baby. It's

Big Truck, Big Trouble

gonna be a boy. I didn't want to leave her this morning because she said she felt a little strange and wondered if today would be the day," Bruce said. They both agreed they needed to get that satellite up the mountain, off the trailer, and secured to the concrete slab that had already been poured.

Hal's weather radio was forecasting heavy late-season snow for later that afternoon, according to the report he had heard on the way over. Hal hoped the report was wrong. Early fall and late spring snow was more than annoying; it was awful. Wet heavy snow makes seeing out the windshield almost impossible, the wiper blades build-up with snow until they look like the "floaties" that the kids use in the swimming pools. They are totally worthless, and he sure didn't need any of that stuff today.

"I'm gonna take my mud flaps off real quick and hang them on the fence here, Bruce, otherwise they'll just end up gettin' torn off on a crummy road like this. Especially, if I have to chain-up, then I can re-install them on my way back out empty. Won't take but a few minutes!"

"That's good thinking," Bruce said.

Then, slowly the two of them started up the rough road. It's times like these when years of experience come into play. Hal knew it wouldn't take very much, just a wrong turn of the steering wheel for a second, to turn this adventure into a tragedy. As Hal eased the big rig up the steep narrow forest road, he thought back to his childhood, how his dad taught him to drive log trucks on roads just like these. "Stay high in the corners, son," his dad used to tell him, "and watch the temperature and oil pressure. You'll cook the engine if you're not careful."

Hal had lost his dad in a logging accident when he was eighteen years old. He

Big Truck, Big Trouble

remembered the funeral service, and how he tried so hard to hold back the tears. It was impossible, his dad meant everything to him. When they weren't working together, they were playing together. Hunting, fishing, swimming, Hal's mom would've had it no other way. Hal lost her to cancer when he was only twelve years old, and after tenth grade, he could take school no longer. Hal's dad tried so hard to keep him in school, but all Hal did in class was draw pictures of the woods and log trucks and no matter what anyone tried he just wouldn't try to study, his heart was not into school. Finally Hal's dad gave in to Hal and let him start working with him in the woods. Hal promised his dad he would get his GED first chance he could but he seemed to forget all about it.Many times, Hal remembered the harsh words the two of them had just before the accident. His dad was running the dozer pulling up a load of saw logs from a steep canyon. Hal told him the slope was too steep, that he needed to lighten the load, but his dad said, "if I wanted your two cents, I'd have asked for it."

"Fine and dandy you old coot," Hal said to his dad. "You just do whatever you think you need to do. I forgot this is your business and your equipment."

Hal had climbed back on the loader and was finishing a log truck when he saw the driver's frantic look as he pointed down the cliff towards Hal's dad. The load of logs had caught on an old stump and pulled the dozer over sideways. Hal kicked the machine into neutral and leaped to the ground, his mind racing. When he got to the edge of the bank his heart sank, the dozer was upside down and the tracks were still turning. "Oh God, please not this, please not my daddy," Hal cried out. But as he reached the overturned dozer, he could see his dad's legs sticking out from

Big Truck, Big Trouble

under it. He raced around the other side and turned off the machine, then dug frantically to get to his dad's head. The roll-cage would have protected his dad, but because he refused to wear the safety belt, he had been knocked out of the driver's seat. Hal put his dad's face in his lap, and slowly he opened his eyes and started to say something.

"Don't try to talk," Hal said with tears streaming down his face.

"Listen to me," his dad said. "I know I'm not gonna make it, and I have to tell you something."

Blood was seeping out from the corners of his mouth, and Hal wiped it with his handkerchief. "You listen to me," Hal said, "you're not going anywhere except to the hospital." Hal knew in his heart his dad didn't have a chance. As the reality of it started to sink in, Hal said, "dad, I love you so much. I didn't mean to talk to you the way I did."

His dad interrupted, "son, I was bull headed and stubborn. I knew you were right about the slope being too steep, but I let my pride get in the way. Listen to me, son. Your momma told me something years ago when she was goin' to be with the Lord. She made me promise to keep you in church and to raise you in a Christian home."

Hal interrupted him, "dad, you did the best you could. I was just never interested in that stuff."

Suddenly, the big rig's front tire fell in a rut, nearly ripping the steering wheel out of Hal's hands. (That's why a driver always keeps his thumbs up to avoid being broken by that very thing.) They don't teach you that in most truck driving schools. Realizing he needed to focus, Hal barked at himself, "Get your mind on what you're doing Dalstrom!. Now's not the time to be

Big Truck, Big Trouble

daydreaming...especially, about stuff like that!"

Hal turned off all the communications equipment he was monitoring, and the country music too, so he could hear the engine and be able to tell when the drive wheels lost traction and started to spin in the deep mud and snow. A quick foot on the throttle and clutch would be in demand soon as the road became rougher and steeper. Around and up, switchback corner after corner, Hal wondered if he should stop and chain-up the drive wheels. But he was still making forward progress, so stopping now might be the worst thing, and to lose the forward momentum he had worked so hard for would be more than a shame; it might be followed by a call to the towing service. And that to Hal, that would be the ultimate defeat.

He could barely see the taillights of the pickup that he was supposed to be following. Bruce was not about to slow down and risk becoming stuck either, but just then they both reached the clearing on top of the ridge. Hal breathed a sigh of relief when he was able to pull the big rig to a halt on somewhat level ground and set the brake. "Well, that wasn't so bad," he hollered out the window to a now grinning Bruce Cotter.

"They said you could do the job, and they weren't kidding," Bruce said with a smile.

"Anytime when we got time, but right now, we ain't got much time," Hal said in his usual sarcastic tone. He stepped out onto the half-frozen ground and started immediately to loosen the strong nylon straps that the loading crew had fastened the satellite to the trailer with. "I'll get the crane started and warmed up, so we can unload this thing, Mr. Dalstrom," Bruce said.

"Please, call me Hal. Only the preacher, the doctor, and the highway

Big Truck, Big Trouble
patrolmen call me Mr. Dalstrom, and they usually want my money," Hal jokingly replied.

A brisk early morning breeze blew through the loosely fitting front door of the dispatch office as Raymond reached for the door handle. He knew by now Hal and Bruce would be at the site. He smiled as he thought about the small part he had played in such an important role. And to think that Cascade Transport had delivered this precious cargo made him feel proud. "Yes, sir, we deliver anything, anywhere, anytime," Raymond bragged to himself as he made his way down the stairway and walked towards the terminal. But when he pulled open the door to the warehouse the bright sunlight spilled into the darkened loading dock area, there by door number one sat a small wooden crate.

Normally, Raymond would not have even given it a second look. Many times, items are left on the docks after the trucks pull out because some of the deliveries are close by and the trucks will double-trip. But this was Saturday, and he knew nothing should be on that dock. As Raymond leaned over and opened the top of the crate his heart sank. There before him was the wiring-harness for the satellite. "Oh no, I can't believe the guys forgot to put this on the truck. What are we gonna do now? Lord, it's times like these when I feel like such a fool, what should I do?" Raymond ran back up the stairs to the dispatch office and quickly dialed Hal's cellphone in the truck. It rang once but a recorded message said, "the cellular customer you have called is unavailable, or has traveled outside the service area."

That great proud moment Raymond had been experiencing earlier, had just turned into a "real bummer," he thought as his head swirled. Not only the reputation of the

Big Truck, Big Trouble

company was at stake, but his supervisory skills were also in question. It was after all, his responsibility to make sure everything on the order was shipped. The silence of the moment was broken by the ring of the telephone. Raymond nearly leaped backwards, it startled him so much.

"Hello, Raymond? This is Annie , and I…"

Raymond interrupted her. "Annie I was just leaving the terminal, and I realized the load crew missed a box of wiring for the satellite. It should have been on Hal's truck."

"Oh my," she said. "What are you gonna do now?"

"Well, I don't have any choice but to throw that box in the back of the blazer and head up there myself. I was thinking of calling Bonnie and see if she would like to go along, at least we could spend some time together," Raymond said.

"Hey, you know what?" Annie asked. "My women's group rummage sale can get by without me today. How about me goin' along and riding back with Hal?"

The huge truck-crane that was waiting on the site coughed and sputtered as Bruce cranked the starter, and the diesel engine roared to life in the cool mountain air. The nearly white overcast sky was filled with the coal-black smoke from the noisy engine. Hal grinned when he heard the big diesel motor make its presence known among the quiet pristine woods. The sound of those big engines always transported him back in time to his early days working with his dad. Hal swung the driver's door open again and reached for his thermos. "Time for one more cup while she warms up," Hal hollered to Bruce. "Come on over and have a doughnut, there fresh this mornin' and real good."

Big Truck, Big Trouble

"Man, it seems like the temperature has dropped ten degrees since we got here," Bruce said.

"Well, that wind ain't helpin' matters either," Hal continued. "The scanner said there's a big storm coming in from the coast this afternoon, and I'm hoping we can get this thing unloaded and fastened down before it hits. They're calling for up to two feet in the mountains." But before Hal and Bruce finished their coffee it started coming down! "Man, 'O Man'," Hal hollered, "will you look at that crap. If it wasn't so pretty, I'd get mad, but we better really get going buddy." Hal threw his thermos bottle in the truck and jumped back down to the ground and scrambled into position.

Bonnie was delighted to hear Raymond's plans as she talked with him on the phone. She loved to get out of the house and go for drives despite the fact that

Stan Surbrook

Raymond was not much of a driver, and he often wondered how guys like Hal could keep from goin' nuts confined to the small cab of the huge trucks they drove. Truth was, Hal could never imagine doing anything else. "That's why the good Lord made so many different species," Hal used to tell his buddies, "so everything will take care of everything else".

After picking up Annie, the three of them stopped by the 'Chicken-Lickin' and got two buckets of mouth-watering barbecue style chicken and all the fixin's. "Boy, are we gonna make a hit with those guys when we pull up with a picnic lunch," Anne said.

"Yeah, and maybe they'll forget all about my little 'boo-boo," Raymond added. "We're gonna have a good time today, and oh yeah, leave the drivin to me," Raymond said with a wink. What he couldn't see was the two

Big Truck, Big Trouble

women's eyes roll, and then Annie said, "well, the Lord will protect us."

You'd never know Hal was fifty-six years old as he leaped off the flatbed trailer and gave a yell, "Take her up, man." Slowly the cable main line tightened as Bruce raised the boom of the crane, "Easy, take it easy," Hal motioned with his hands. The trailer's suspension groaned and gave a pop or two as the load was lifted from it. Hal loved to hear that sound because it signaled to him that his job was almost done. Soon he would be heading down this mountain and back to more familiar territory. Hal would deny it, but he'd had a bad feeling about this load ever since Raymond called him on the phone last week. "Just your imagination running away with you," Hal argued with himself. Still, he would be glad to see the on-ramp of the interstate and the last of this mountain.

"Good gravy," Raymond said as he shrugged his shoulders, "this is the pits. We're not gonna get there 'till way after dark at this speed."

"Well, honey, you just might as well get your blood-pressure back down because I don't think we're going anywhere for a long time," Bonnie said, trying to ease the tension of the moment. The three of them had been caught behind a truck accident and both lanes of the interstate were plugged solid.

"Well, pass me some of that 'Chicken-Lickin' and a couple of biscuits," Raymond said with a lot of effort, trying his hardest to appear calm. "Dear Lord," Raymond said as he bowed his head, "thank you for this food we are fixin' to eat, and please Lord, help us get through this traffic quickly, and please take care of Bruce and Hal. We ask this in Jesus' name. Amen." Annie and Bonnie both said a loud 'Amen' as

Big Truck, Big Trouble

they, too, reached into the 'Chicken-Lickin' bag.

About halfway between the trailer and the concrete slab where the satellite would sit on, Bruce suddenly stopped. Hal's attention focused on the young man as he shut down the machine and grabbed his cell phone from his belt. "Hello, this is Bruce," the caller was 'breaking-up' and there was a lot of static on the line.

"Hello, are you there?" The caller's voice became clear enough for Bruce to understand, "this is Sue, your neighbor from across the street. Holly fell and hit her head. We're taking her to the emergency room." Hal was close enough to see the expression on Bruce's face through the glass windows of the crane's cab, and he looked very troubled. "Holly said please hurry, but be careful." The signal grew too weak to hear anything but static, and when it cleared, the caller had hung up. Bruce Flung open the door of the crane with such force that it nearly left the hinges and didn't even take time to dismount the machine by way of the metal ladder but instead took one giant leap; his feet were already moving before they touched the ground.

"My wife…my wife fell down and I gotta go," Bruce yelled at Hal.

"You'll have to finish up here by yourself," Bruce said nervously. "I'm sorry, but I have to go…the baby."

Hal held up a hand, "hey now, just calm down, you can't do anything unless you calm down," Hal told him.

"Alright, you're right, I'm okay, I just… I can pray, and that's what I'll do, just pray and drive."

"Don't worry about anything here," Hal said reassuringly, "I can run this little 'ol crane, no sweat."

Big Truck, Big Trouble

"Thank you so much, Mr. Dalstrom."

Snow was really beginning to fly as Bruce cranked the pickup's engine and then mashed the accelerator pedal sending a barrage of mud allover the side of the crane. Hal watched as the pickup headed down the steep rugged trail bouncing and turning until the taillights faded out of sight. He climbed up the ladder to the one hundred twenty-foot truck crane that the satellite company had rented and switched the key to engage the starter of the big diesel engine. Smoke billowed from the stubby exhaust pipe of the machine, as Hal grinned and thought, "This is just like old times." He was daydreaming again about his time as a young lad in the woods with his dad.

It's not so easy to place an object of this size on a few small bolts that are sticking up out of a concrete slab by yourself unless you happen to be a real good operator. Let alone in a wind-driven snowstorm. But as Hal maneuvered the huge crane into position, the 'feel of the stick' came back to him. Some things you never forget how to do, no matter how many years go by, and this was no exception. Hal was, in his youth, an excellent operator. His dad had taught him well, years ago deep in the woods. He started to take Hal to work with him when he was just six years old and would set him on his lap and place his little hands on the control levers along with his, to teach him the 'feel' of the machines. Hal loved his dad's big strong hands.

However, it took Hal more than an hour to get the huge dish in place and to attach the bolts and nuts 'hand-tightened'. He couldn't do much more than that since he had only a limited number of tools available to him. Besides, he knew that the hook-up crew would be there first thing Monday morning, and they would do the rest. So, he retracted

Big Truck, Big Trouble

the telescoping boom of the machine, shut it down and locked the cranes' cab door, placing the key on top of the battery box that was hidden under the cowling of the engine cover. This was a common practice of heavy equipment operators, and Hal knew the men would know just where to locate it come Monday morning.

The light of day was almost gone as Hal warmed-up the big rig's engine and he wished he was already back down to the main road and headed for home. But he knew the first thing that he had to do was to get the drive wheels chained-up, and that took a half-hour of cold wet work, so after that, he sat in the cab of the truck with the heater on high and finally got warmed back up. But as he let the clutch out the drive tires lost traction and started to slip. Hal knew exactly what was wrong. The trailer's brake shoes had frozen to the drums and the only way to free them would require him to crawl under the trailer and 'hammer' them free from the drums. He grabbed the hammer from his toolbox and climbed back out of his truck and gave the door a slam unaware of the heavy wet snow that had already accumulated on the roof of the truck and down it came, with such force it nearly knocked him to the ground. The wet cold stuff went right down his collar and startled him enough that he cursed himself for being so stupid. "That's exactly what you get Dalstrom, what stupid thing are you gonna do next?" Hal asked himself.

After a few minutes of hard work, Hal was heading down the rough, crooked road. It looked so much different now that it was dark, and the heavy wet snow made it almost impossible to see. The windshield wipers seem to 'plug-up' with the white slime, and Hal found himself straining to focus as he leaned forward to see through the windshield.

Big Truck, Big Trouble

"I don't need this right now," Hal shouted out loud. "How much further to the paved road. I don't remember any of this."

"I can't believe it's taken us more than three hours to go a hundred miles," Raymond said, shaking his head. "Annie , hand me the cell phone, and I'll try to call them one more time." Raymond couldn't understand why Bruce wasn't answering his phone. The reception was marginal at best, but the calls were going through, yet all he heard was ring, and ring, and ring. "I don't know why I can't get through to them," Raymond told Annie and Bonnie, "something doesn't feel right to me."

"I don't think we'll see them going the other way now either, because it's too dark to see the other side of the interstate," Bonnie said but then quickly added, "but I know the Lord is in control."

"Well regardless," answered Raymond, "we still have to drop off this stuff that was supposed to be on the truck. I was just hoping we could beat the weather. Did you see what the 'pass condition sign' back there said?"

"Yes, I sure did," said Annie.

Raymond thought about what the sign had read: 'heavy blowing snow with poor visibility, chains required.' Then he said quietly to himself, "Dear Lord, if they're still up there, they could be in big trouble."

Hal was about half way down to the paved road when he was completely blinded by the blowing snow. He mashed hard on the brakes but felt the big rig skid as the trailer started to 'jack-knife'. He knew he had to get off the brakes fast and give a little gas, but he couldn't see, but just then he saw what looked like tire tracks in the fresh snow. "Yes, yes," Hal said with a smile, "it's Bruce's tire tracks.

Big Truck, Big Trouble

All I gotta do now is follow these babies to freedom!"

Even though he could only see two feet in front of the rig, Hal breathed a sigh of relief because he figured he could 'feel' his way out to the pavement now. But all of a sudden, the truck dipped from side to side and then he felt the front end drop a couple of feet and he found himself once again 'standing on' the brakes. He instinctively glanced in the left mirror to watch helplessly as the trailer 'came around' from the left side and slid off the edge of the narrow road. He knew he had to floor the accelerator and use the forward momentum to pull the trailer back up on the road, but he couldn't see ahead anymore and the tracks he had been following were gone. "Oh God help me," he said as he mashed the throttle, glancing quickly in the left mirror to watch the trailer come back up on the road. But when he swung his head back forward, he saw a dark object in the dim headlights. He yanked the steering wheel to the left to miss it and then saw nothing but pure white light from the headlights. "That's it," he hollered out as he pushed hard on the brakes, but it wouldn't stop. He felt the ground below him give way and the entire rig plunged headlong down a steep cliff.

Hal's eyes opened to the sound of the 'engine warning buzzer' and a sharp pain in his left leg. "What the…," Hal breathed out and the pain nearly made him pass out again. He reached up and found the steering wheel and felt it down to the key and turned the ignition off. His head was spinning, and he felt sick to his stomach. He dropped his left arm down to feel his leg and suddenly realized why it hurt so bad. When he pulled his hand back, he could see blood and he reached frantically with his right arm to find the dome light.

Big Truck, Big Trouble

The cold was almost unbearable as he gave the dome light switch a turn, and when the light came on Hal realized the horror of it all. The rig had slid about seventy-five feet down a rocky slope and in the process, the trailer had turned completely upside down forcing the truck to roll over on the left side. Hal's leg was badly broken, and it took a few seconds before he had the nerve to look down at the mess. "You're okay," he told himself, as he forced his eyes to look down at the twisted remains of what used to be his left leg. The door had been smashed in like a pop can, but the seat had stayed put, pinning his leg and breaking it under the extreme pressure.

The bone was sticking out and it hurt him something awful. Hal tried desperately to remain calm and was reminded of the many times he had come across car wrecks on the freeway and how he had told people, "stay calm, it'll be alright." But this was different, much different. Hal knew the first thing he must do to prevent shock was to stay warm. He grabbed the shift knob and quickly found 'neutral' position in the transmission then gave the engine a crank. Surprisingly, it fired right up, but Hal knew it wouldn't run long on the angle he was setting because the engine oil would run out the 'oil fill' pipe. And without oil the engine would not run and the automatic shutdown would occur so he only had about two or maybe three minutes of run time.

"Okay, okay," Hal thought to himself, "this isn't that bad. I'll just rest here for a minute or two and then we'll take charge of the situation." Hal was starting to shiver as the cold wet snow blew through the gaping hole where the door hinges had been ripped away. The heater was on full blast, but it wasn't doing much to warm the cab, and Hal knew how fast the temperature could drop up here in the mountains at night. He reached as far as he

Big Truck, Big Trouble

could but was still six inches too short from taking hold of the cell phone. "I can't believe that stupid thing stayed hooked on the dash, any other time it falls off at the slightest bump." Since the truck was laying on its left side, the right side of the dashboard was now straight up. "If that phone would've just fell off like it always does, it would be right here by me. That's just some more of my rotten luck."

Hal knew what he had to do if he was going to survive. He had to free himself from the seat, get that leg splinted and stop the bleeding. Then he would try to get some help. Maybe the cell phone would work well enough to call 911 and maybe, just maybe he would make it out of this little jam to tell his grandkids all about it. Suddenly the engine warning buzzer came on again and Hal looked at the oil pressure gauge and realized the engine would automatically shut down soon because the pressure was nearly gone. Sure enough, it shut down within a minute and Hal tried the starter once again, but it would no longer run. Hal knew he had to shut off all the lights to save the battery, so he could use the cell phone after he freed himself. But before he did, he reached up and wiped the inside of the windshield so he could see ahead of him. The snow had stopped momentarily, and as the headlights illuminated the steep cliff side that he had mistakenly driven off, he couldn't believe his eyes. There at the bottom of the canyon was the crumpled-up wreck of Bruce's pick-up truck. The tail-lights were still lit but Hal knew Bruce could not have survived that fall.

Now it all made sense, he had been following Bruce's tracks all right, but Bruce had got confused and turned left down the old mine road and the both of them had plummeted off the side of the mountain. Hal

Big Truck, Big Trouble

was just sick, Bruce was no doubt dead, and no one would be looking for them before morning, and Hal knew they would find him dead as well. "I can't believe this," Hal said aloud. The pain in his leg was throbbing now and Hal thought, "I'm not gonna die up here on this mountain, not like this." He switched off the headlights leaving only the dome light on in the cab. Then he got a napkin out of his lunch pail, which was now lying beside him, with everything else, and put it in his mouth to bite down on. The seat was air operated and Hal knew if he released all the air from it, he might be able to pull his broken, twisted leg free.

Hal counted to ten and pulled the button on the base of the seat to lower it. He bit down hard and pulled with all his might. He expected it to hurt bad, but he had no idea of the pain he was about to encounter. He felt a warm rush to his face and immediately became nauseous as the blood-soaked limb pulled out of the entrapment. He was free of the seat but unable to move anywhere, at least for now. Blood was spurting from just above his knee, the result of a deep cut from the sheet metal in the door. He took the napkin from his mouth and pushed down hard on the gushing wound. "Okay now," Hal said to himself, "just rest a little now. Get the bleeding stopped, then, get it splinted."

An hour and a half had gone by since the accident had first happened, and Hal had made little progress. The cold had taken its toll on his body. His fingers felt like they were two inches around as he struggled to tie pieces of rope around the 'highway flares' he had placed on each side of his leg for a makeshift splint. It wasn't perfect but it worked well enough to let him position his body enough to get hold of the cell phone. He had a hard time pushing the buttons on the phone since by now

Big Truck, Big Trouble

he had lost most of the feeling in his fingers and they were starting to turn blue. But when he finally did punch in 911, the phone did not respond. He frantically tried the number again…nothing; not a sound came from the phone. Hal fell back against the side of the seat exhausted, frustrated, but not defeated.

"I'm not gonna die like this!" Hal said it over and over again trying to convince himself. He grabbed the big hammer from the toolbox and started to beat on the windshield, pieces of glass flying everywhere. He had to stop and rest his arm a few times but before long he had a way of escape. But escape to where? He knew he didn't have the strength to climb up the steep snow-covered rocks and maybe leaving the cab of the truck was a terrible mistake, at least it provided some shelter. But he had to do something, even if it was wrong, he just couldn't sit there waiting for the end. He knew he had to get down to where Bruce's pickup truck was, there was a chance he was still alive. Before he left the truck, he dug in his toolbox once again finding a roll of duct tape. "Good old duct tape, strong and sticky" Hal said out loud, trying hard to find some humor in the desperate moment. He held his breath as he began to wrap it around the highway flares, the cloth napkin, and the pieces of rope that circled his mangled leg. He didn't stop until he had applied the entire roll to his leg.

There's no way Hal could've prepared himself for what happened next. As he exited the truck through the busted-out windshield, his right boot caught on a piece of metal window trim, and he couldn't put enough weight on his bad leg to keep him upright. His body slammed down face first into the rocky hillside cutting a gash in his forehead. But that was just the start of the wild ride he was about to take. As he rolled onto his back, he started

Big Truck, Big Trouble

to slip down the hillside. He clawed desperately with his hands in the frozen ground to grab hold but could not stop his fall. He slid feet first until the injured leg hit a pile of rocks and he started to roll over sideways. He screamed with pain as he rolled over and over descending the remaining twenty-five feet to the canyon's floor and landing right beside Bruce's beat-up truck.

Hal had again been knocked unconscious and lay there in the snow for ten minutes before waking up. When he did, he had a mouthful of snow and even though he knew it could speed hypothermia to eat it, he couldn't resist. His body needed fluids badly and he knew anything about now would help. The silence was broken by a faint moan. Hal couldn't believe his ears. "Bruce, are you alright?" Hal asked, almost forgetting about his own injuries.

"Oh, thank you, Lord. Mr. Dalstrom, is that you?" Bruce asked in a soft voice.

"Bruce, I'm kinda busted up a little, but don't you worry, everything's gonna be just fine." Hal felt better already despite his condition, at least he wasn't alone.

"I guess we should've just stayed home," Raymond said hopelessly. "First we get delayed for two and a half hours by a truck wreck, then they close the pass for three more hours. It'll be daylight by the time we get back home, and we've still gotta drop this stuff off, and worst of all I'm not even sure we can get up that road now, not after all this snow."

"All I wanted to do was to ride home with Hal. He's probably home right now wondering where in the world I am," said a tired and disgusted Annie. "I'll try dialing Hal's cell phone number once again."

"Still no answer?" Raymond asked her.

Big Truck, Big Trouble

"No, and I don't understand it either. Hal always calls, at least when he gets hungry, and I know by now, he's hungry!

It about killed him, but Hal managed to pull his bruised, busted-up body closer to the crumpled remains of what used to be Bruce Cotter's pickup truck. "Bruce, listen man," Hal tried to sound in charge of the situation, "we're gonna be fine, just fine. All we gotta do is hang in there for a little while and they'll be comin' to get us." Hal knew that wasn't the truth; the truth was that no one would even miss them for hours, hours they didn't have. Hal wondered how much more he could actually take. And what about Bruce, he hadn't even got a look at Bruce. "Uh, listen Bruce, how bad of shape are you, can you walk?" Up to this point Hal had kept a pretty good rein on his emotions and was trying his best to remain calm, but the tragedy of the moment was overwhelming. He knew that they were in trouble and unless things started getting better real soon, they would never make it off that mountain.

The weather had 'backed-off' just a bit and the moon was trying to peak out from behind the soft white clouds. As Hal lay there on his back in the snow he gazed into the beauty of that wonderfully full moon and for a fleeing moment remembered how his sweet Annie loved to lay out back on the deck of their house on those warm summer evenings and watch the heavens. She would softly say to him, "someday, Jesus will come back in all his glory, and we'll go home to live with him forever." Hal was really missing her as he thought about her tender touch; how he longed to see her again.

But reality set back in when a rock fell from where the big rig was perched high above them and narrowly missed him. Hal knew he had to get to Bruce fast because he

Big Truck, Big Trouble

didn't know how long it would be before that hillside let loose of its grip, and the whole thing would come crashing down on them both.

He inched his way closer to Bruce's pickup truck while talking to him but the words that Bruce spoke were slurred and heavy. Hal wondered what he would see when he did get to Bruce. And wished he didn't have to do this; he had been through enough. He couldn't even take care of himself, let alone help this man who obliviously was hurt worse than he. But soon Hal was looking poor Bruce right in the eyes. He was hurt worse than Hal could have imagined. And since he wasn't wearing his seatbelt either, gravity had taken over. Bruce's chest had hit the steering wheel with such force that it snapped in half like a pretzel. Hal was sure the impact alone would've produced broken ribs in the least, but the lacerations to his face and forehead were ghastly.

"Bruce, you may not feel like it right now, but you're gonna be alright. We're gonna come out of this thing okay," said a weary Hal Dalstrom.

"Mr. Dalstrom," Bruce answered. "Well, I guess we can use first names now, we sorta have something in common." Bruce was digging around with his right arm and Hal assumed he was attempting to free himself from the wreckage. "Now just sit tight there Bruce, the paramedics will be here in a few minutes. All we have to do is hang on, just for a little while longer," Hal said to him softly

Finally, Raymond took the "Railroad Canyon Road" exit off the snow-covered interstate and headed up the two-lane road. He wondered to himself why there were no fresh tracks in the snow, "Boy, it must have really dumped up here to cover Hal's tracks over."

Big Truck, Big Trouble

But when they reached the gate Raymond's heart sank. And it must have showed on his face because Anne immediately asked, "what's wrong, Ray?"

"What's wrong is, they're still in there," said Raymond.

"What? How do you know that, Ray?" Bonnie asked, hoping Raymond was wrong.

"See those mud flaps hanging on the fence? Those are Hal's, he took them off here at the gate, because he knew he would just end up tearing them off on a rough road like this. And look at the lock, it's hooked on the inside of the gate!"

"Mr. Dalstrom, Hal I mean, please help me get…"

"Don't try to move," Hal interrupted.

"No, please, help me get hold of my…I can't reach it," Bruce pleaded.

Hal struggled to get closer to him and got his good leg under him enough to push his

[70]

body up to where Bruce was, still behind the wheel of the pickup truck, but pinned under the steering column and what used to be the dashboard of the truck. "I can't believe this thing landed right-side up," Hal said aloud.

Hal could see good enough by the full moon to find what Bruce had been looking for. There was a lot of blood around Bruce; mostly, it looked to Hal, coming from the nasty cuts on Bruce's face. "Here 'ya go, Bruce," Hal said but at the same time realizing that Bruce couldn't see a thing. His face was so swollen, it looked like a time years ago when Hal's dad had turned over an old stump in the woods and exposed a bunch of hornets that were getting ready to winter there. Hal's dad got stung twenty-two times and nearly had an allergic reaction. "Uh, Bruce, I guess you just want to hold it a while…"

"No, please, Hal…you read it to me."

Big Truck, Big Trouble

"Oh, well, Bruce…I mean I'm not much of a reader anyway, and I sure don't think I could do the 'Good Book' much justice with all the 'thee's and tho's' and all of that," Hal said apologetically.

"Listen to me, please, Hal. I know I'm hurt bad, and I don't think I'm gonna make it. I can feel my life slipping away."

"Now just stop that kinda takin' right now," Hal said with authority.

"Please, read me the twenty-third psalm."

"The what?" Hal asked.]

"Psalms…just look in the front, the index, Hal, and then turn to the one that says Psalm twenty-three."

Hal labored with half-frozen fingers to turn the pages to find the scripture Bruce was looking for. "Here it is, Bruce," Hal said squinting in the moon light to see the small print. He suddenly thought to try the dome light of the pickup truck and was amazed that it still worked. However, the added light revealed just how badly hurt poor Bruce was. His color was snow white and his body quivered with rhythmic shivers. Hal thought little of his own injuries now and wished there was something he could do for the man.

"Hal…Mr. Dalstrom, please read it to me," Bruce begged.

"Ah…ok, here goes. The Lord is my shepherd, I shall not be in want." Hal paused and looked to Bruce for approval much like a school mate looks to his teacher. Bruce sat motionless, his body captive of the crushed steering column.

"Please keep reading," Bruce pleaded.

"He makes me lie down in green pastures, he leads me beside still waters. He restores my soul." Something was happening…to both of them. Bruce stopped shivering, and Hal felt a sense of peace. "He

Big Truck, Big Trouble

guides me in the path of righteousness for his name's sake," Hal read on. "Even though I walk through the valley of the shadow of death, I will fear no evil, for you are with me; your rod and your staff, they comfort me. You prepare a table before me in the presence of my enemies. You anoint my head with oil; my cup overflows. Surely goodness and love will follow me all the days of my life, and I will dwell in the house of the Lord forever."

"Hal, do you realize how much the Father loves us? Do you really know where you are going when you die?" Suddenly, like no time before Hal thought about that question. The sense of not really knowing if he would make it off that mountain or not, brought the question of eternity sharply into focus. Hal remembered his dad pinned under the overturned bulldozer, and that he had asked Hal that very question.

"Well, Bruce, I..."

"Listen, Hal, it doesn't matter what you have, or have not done. Jesus died for my sins, for yours, for everybody's. He paid the ultimate price, his life. He shed his precious blood for all our sins. All you have to do, right now is just admit you need him in your life, ask the Father to forgive you, believe with your heart and confess with your mouth that Jesus Christ is Lord of all and immediately he will forgive you. The scriptures say that God doesn't want anyone to perish, but that all would have everlasting life…in heaven, Hal."

Suddenly some small rocks came rolling down from where the twisted remains of the big rig came to rest. Hal looked up and saw some more rocks and dirt start to give way. "Bruce, we gotta get out of here."

"Remember what I told you, Hal…please." Hal couldn't believe what happened next. The large boulder that had stopped the big rig from falling to the

Big Truck, Big Trouble

canyon's floor pushed out and with an awesome groan the whole thing came sliding down the hillside, picking up speed as it lunged forward smashing everything in its path. Hal looked at poor Bruce and realized there was no way short of a miracle for the huge truck to miss him. Hal didn't want to leave him but at the last-minute, Hal rolled over and over, pain gashing up his leg, but fear propelled him. Then, he saw the big rig strike the pickup truck. It hit with such force that it looked like a hundred-pound sack of potatoes dropped on a pop can. "Bruce, oh no…please." Just then the spare tire that was in the bed of the pickup truck came crashing down on Hal's head, once again knocking him unconscious, but this time causing severe head trauma.

Six days later off the ventilator but still in a coma, Hal lay in a ICU hospital bed with five broken ribs, a punctured spleen and a couple cracked vertebrae in his neck, his right leg in a cast and a bandage on his head. Annie sat by his bedside reading her bible and rubbing Hal's foot. "Hal, sweetheart, please wake up…I know you can pull through this one, you're as tough as nails. Hal, I need you." Then Annie dropped her head and prayed, "Dear Lord, please Lord, I need Hal in my life. I know you'll always take care of me Lord, but I also know that you gave this man to me, to help me oh Lord, please bring him back to me…please."

Suddenly, Hal coughed a couple of times and then started to mumble something as he fought to open his eyes. "Thank you, Lord," Annie said out loud as she pushed the 'call' button on the side of Hal's bed; and a nurse showed up almost immediately.

"Yes, ma'am, can I help you?"

"He's waking up," Annie said, her eyes now filled with tears.

Big Truck, Big Trouble

"I'll get doctor Owens," replied the nurse as she hurried out of the room.

Doctor Owens had already begun to examine Hal before he was completely awake. "Well, good morning, Mr. Dalstrom. How are you feeling?" the doctor asked.

Hal's raspy voice never sounded so good to Annie as he answered the doctor's question, "I've been better, I've been worse. What happened, wa...where am I..."

"Now take it easy, big boy," the doctor said smiling, "you've been in the hospital for a few days. You were in an accident but you're gonna be just fine. You've got a great little woman here who loves you and will tell you everything you want to know in just a minute. But right now, I want you to take some deep breaths for me."

Hal let out a yelp as the doctor pulled him forward and slapped the cold stethoscope on his back. "Nothin' wrong with your feelings," the doctor said with a grin.

Annie sat on the bed next to Hal as the two of them embraced each other for nearly a half hour after the doctor left the room. Tears were plentiful as Annie helped Hal remember the events that had taken place that awful night, now nearly a week earlier. "I know he's in heaven, with the Lord, Annie," Hal said, still having trouble forming words. "I believe, too, Annie . Bruce said the same stuff you've told me about a thousand times, but I finally realized how quickly your life can be gone. That's when I asked Jesus to wash my sins away and to come into my heart. If I would've come off that mountain the same way Bruce did, I know where I'd be right now, and I know where I would spend eternity."

Annie treasured these things in her heart as she held tight her lifelong friend and

Big Truck, Big Trouble

listened to everything that he said. "Oh thank you Lord, thank you," Annie said to herself.

Hal spent another seven days in the hospital before he finally got to go home. And it was none too soon either. He might have got a 'tune-up' spiritually, but he was still Hal. A lifetime of doing his 'own thing' would take a while to change, and he was thankful for that. He also knew his life would be much different now without that leg, and his long career on the road was over, but instead of being bitter, he was thankful. Thankful for his new life, and thankful for his precious little wife.

Stan Surbrook

A note from the author

If this little story has in some way touched your heart; and you would like to know more about how you, too, can be free from your sins by believing and putting your faith in Jesus Christ, feel free to email me at:

www.chappie777@comcast.net

Big Truck, Big Trouble

www.ingramcontent.com/pod-product-compliance
Lightning Source LLC
Chambersburg PA
CBHW071422070526
44578CB00003B/658